LINCOLNWOOD PUBLIC LIBRARY

W9-ANT-814

Lincolnwood Library
4000 W. Pratt Ave.
Lincolnwood, IL 60712

DOWN SYNDROME

J
616.858
BRI

DOWN SYNDROME

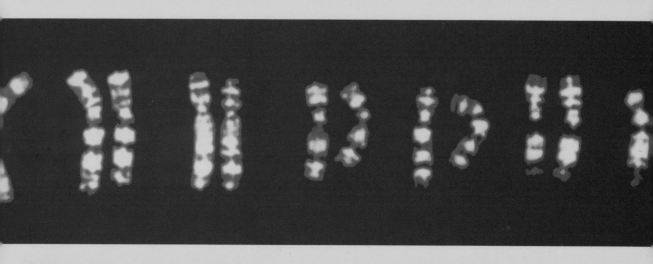

Marlene Targ Brill

 **Marshall Cavendish**
Benchmark
New York

The author is grateful to Alison Brill, Christy Cook, Emily Kingsley, Julie Rowe, and Linda Moran for sharing their experiences with Down syndrome.

With thanks to Dr. Laura Cifra-Bean, a pediatrician with Lake Hospitals and a director of the National Down Sydrome Congress. Laura and her husband, Andy, have three children, and her son Christopher has Down syndrome. Her practice includes providing care for many patients with Down syndrome, the part of her job that she loves most.

Special thanks to Sue Joe, Resource Specialist, of the National Down Syndrome Congress for her invaluable help with this book.

Marshall Cavendish Benchmark
99 White Plains road
Tarrytown, New York 10591-9001
www.marshallcavendish.us

Text copyright © 2007 by Marshall Cavendish Corporation

All rights reserved. No part of this book may be reproduced or utilized in any form or by any means electronic or mechanical including photocopying, recording, or by any information storage and retrieval system, without permission from the copyright holders.

This book is not intended for use as a substitute for advice, consultation, or treatment by a licensed medical practitioner. The reader is advised that no action of a medical nature should be taken without consultation with a licensed medical practitioner, including action that may seem to be indicated by the contents of this work, since individual circumstances vary and medical standards, knowledge, and practices change with time. The publisher, author, and medical consultants disclaim all liability and cannot be held responsible for any problems that may arise from the use of this book.

Library of Congress Cataloging-in-Publication Data

Brill, Marlene Targ.
  Down syndrome / by Marlene Targ Brill.
     p. cm. -- (Health alert)
  Summary: "Explores the history, causes, symptoms, treatments, and future
of Down syndrome"--Provided by publisher.
  Includes bibliographical references and index.
  ISBN-13: 978-0-7614-2207-5
  ISBN-10: 0-7614-2207-2
  1. Down syndrome--Juvenile literature. I. Title. II. Series: Health alert
(New York, N.Y.)

  RC571.B69 2007
  616.85'8842--dc22

                                    2006015817

Photo research by Candlepants, Incorporated
Front cover: A karyotype image showing chromosomes in Down syndrome.
Title page: This image, called a karyotype, shows chromosomes arranged in pairs.
Front cover: Dr. Dennis Kunkel/PhototakeUSA.com
The photographs in this book are used by permission and through the courtesy of:
Photo Researchers Inc.: Chris Bjornberg, 3, 12,: / L. Willatt/East Anglian Regional Genetics Service, 5, 30; Petit Format, 11; Laurant ; American Hospital in Paris, 13; Lauren Shear, 15, 36, 38; Gary Parker, 40; Bruce Roberts, 17; Susan Leavines, 19; Richard J. Green, 28; James King-Holmes, 31; Hattie Young, 34, 46; Richard Hutchings, 43, 48; Elaine Rebman, 45; Lawrence Migdale, 47. *Corbis*: LWA-Dann Tardif, 21; Jerry Cooke, 25; Laura Dwight, 33; Tim Garcha/zefa, 49; Mika/zefa, 52, 55. *The Langdon Down Centre Trust*: 27. *Laura Dwight/Peter Arnold Inc.*: 37. *PhotofestNYC.com*: 56 (top). *Alyce Sosnowski*: 56 (bottom). *Harcort Brace & Company Photo by Richard Hutchings*: 57
Printed in China

6 5 4 3 2 1

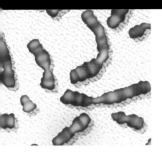

CONTENTS

Chapter 1   What Is It Like to Have Down Syndrome?   6

Chapter 2   What Is Down Syndrome?   10

Chapter 3   The History of Down Syndrome   24

Chapter 4   Living with Down Syndrome   32

Glossary   58

Find Out More   60

Index   63

WHAT IS IT LIKE TO HAVE DOWN SYNDROME?

Tammy could not wait to meet Jake, her new baby brother. When he came home from the hospital, Jake turned out to be as cute as Tammy had imagined. One thing surprised Tammy, though. Jake did not look like her or either of her parents. His nose seemed flat. His pink tongue peeked out of his mouth and seemed too big for the opening. He had almond-shaped eyes and loose skin folds gathered on the back of his short neck.

Tammy loved having a new baby in the house. She talked softly to Jake and begged her mother to hold him. Her parents tried to act as excited as Tammy was. But something seemed wrong. When Tammy left the room, her parents spoke in hushed voices so she could not hear what they were saying. They stopped whispering when she returned. What was the big secret? Tammy could not understand why her parents were so worried about their new baby.

A few days after Jake came home, Tammy's parents sat down

with her. Her father told her that Jake had a condition called Down syndrome. This made him different from most other babies, Tammy's dad explained. He said that Down syndrome was something Jake was born with, like his black hair and brown eyes. He asked whether Tammy had noticed the extra fold of skin covering the inner corners of Jake's eyes or the odd crease across the palms of his hands. These and his other unusual features were outward signs of Down syndrome.

Tammy's mother explained that some children with Down syndrome also have health problems that cannot be seen. In fact, Jake did have a heart problem, but it would probably go away with time. Tammy began to understand why her parents had seemed worried about something ever since Jake was born.

No one knew yet what Down syndrome would mean for Jake and the family. The family pediatrician had told Tammy's parents that children with Down syndrome grow up with a range of different skills. Jake would probably learn at a slower rate and need much more help than other babies. Tammy's parents said they would do everything to give Jake the best possible start in life.

Jake soon became a loving part of the family. In many ways, he was like a regular baby. He smiled, cried, and needed to have his diaper changed every few hours. But he was different from most babies as well. Jake had trouble eating and moving around. His muscles were weak, so he was not able to raise himself with his hands at a time when most babies develop strong arms. His head flopped for months, and he turned over and sat by himself later than most babies his age. Feeding took a long time because Jake's large, round tongue pushed the bottle back out of his mouth.

Jake required extra work from everyone. He had to visit more doctors because his heart problem needed to be monitored. He saw different **therapists,** who helped him strengthen his muscles and encouraged his talking. He needed constant activity to help him develop overall. Still, Tammy and her parents cheered Jake on whenever he learned something new. They clapped when Jake began to walk at twenty-two months, which was about four months later than the range for most babies.

Tammy tried to help, and she loved Jake. But sometimes she wished for her old life back, the one before Jake arrived. She wanted to go out more with her friends. And she wanted to spend more time with her parents doing all the things they had done before Jake came into their lives. They were so busy with Jake, there was not much time to go to the movies or skating or hiking the way they used to.

But Tammy would not have traded Jake for anything. She loved watching him learn new things. When Jake was old enough to walk and move his fingers, the speech therapist taught Jake and the rest of the family some hand signs. It was fun using these hand signs to communicate with Jake until he learned to talk.

Slowly, Jake began to say words and short sentences. His heart problem corrected itself. He could use the bathroom by himself at about age five. By the time he started kindergarten at the same elementary school Tammy had gone to, Jake could care for himself away from home.

By fourth grade, he took some classes with other students who had special needs. But he took gym, music, and art classes with kids from nondisabled classes. He learned to read simple sentences and to count money and tell time. Outside school, he took part in the Special Olympics. His favorite sports were running relays and jumping.

By the time Tammy went away to college, she and Jake were close. She missed him whenever she was away. She wondered about Jake's future. Would he go to college, too? Would he be able to live on his own or in a group home with other adults who had special needs? Would he find work? Tammy knew that, just like healthy kids, every child with Down syndrome was unique. The intelligence and abilities of kids with Down syndrome could range from very slow to normal. There was no telling what Jake would achieve by the time he became an adult.

2

WHAT IS DOWN SYNDROME?

Down syndrome (DS) is a condition that changes a baby's physical and mental development. These changes may result in short fingers, slanted eyes, deeply creased palms, and other different traits. Down syndrome is the leading cause of **mental retardation,** which means learning at a slower than average pace. The term **syndrome** is used to describe a set of features that appear together and point to a condition. Babies who have DS are born with it. Their condition is not an illness like the flu, and no one can catch DS from them.

The condition occurs in every race, religion, and economic level. Children with DS come from every nation in the world. Each year about 4,000 infants are born with Down syndrome in the United States. The National Down Syndrome Society claims that more than 350,000 people with DS live in the United States alone.

GENETICS AND THE BODY

Down syndrome is part of **human genetics,** the basic makeup of the body. To understand Down syndrome, it is helpful to

Children with Down syndrome may have some different physical features than other family members, but they share many feelings, interests, and experiences.

know a few things about genetics. The human body is made of millions of tiny **cells** that begin to form and multiply as a **fetus** develops before it is born. Each fetal cell determines growth and physical characteristics, such as height, voice quality, eye, and hair color. Message centers in the cells called **genes** govern these characteristics. Genes include all the details for how human bodies develop before and after birth.

Genes look like tiny threadlike rods. They are so small, they can be seen only through a powerful microscope. Genes are located in parts of cells called **chromosomes.** Usually, there are 46 chromosomes in every human cell. The chromosomes are arranged into 23 pairs. Scientists have numbered each pair from 1 to 23 in order to study and remember them more easily.

Genes offer clues about how features are passed from parent to child. A baby's genes come from both parents. One chromosome of each pair is from the mother. The other chromosome in each pair comes from the father. The pairs work together to

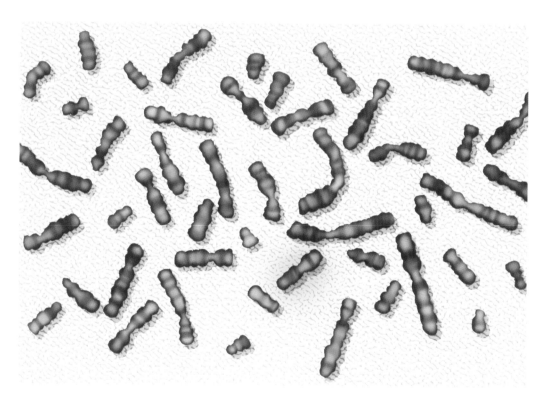

The extra copy of chromosome 21, shown here in green, causes most cases of Down syndrome.

Types of Down Syndrome

Trisomy 21
About 95 out of 100 children with DS have an extra chromosome in pair 21. The extra cell creates three chromosomes, rather than the usual two. Scientists call this type of chromosome mistake trisomy. *Tri* means three and *somy* refers to chromosomes.

Translocation
Two other errors also involve chromosome 21. A child may have the normal number of chromosomes—46—but chromosome 21 has an extra part. When this abnormal chromosome 21 changes location, or translocates, Down syndrome develops.

Mosaicism
In a form of Down syndrome called mosaicism, cells contain mixed numbers of chromosomes. Some have 46 chromosomes and some have 47. Both translocation and mosaicism account for only 4 to 5 percent of DS cases.

Each type of Down syndrome involves an extra chromosome. Except in mosaicism, the extra chromosome becomes part of every cell in the body. One extra chromosome is enough to block normal development of body parts and the brain. That is why children with DS may look different from other children. They may be more likely to have certain birth defects or illnesses, or they may develop more slowly. The range of problems varies with each child.

A trisomy 21 researcher investigates the cause and timing of errors in cell division that lead to Down syndrome.

help cells divide and multiply into the cells of different parts of a body.

Sometimes, an accident occurs during cell division when chromosomes copy themselves. Sometimes the copy ends up with an extra chromosome. Babies born with this extra, or forty-seventh, chromosome in each of their cells have Down syndrome.

WHAT ARE SIGNS OF DOWN SYNDROME?

Doctors usually notice signs of Down syndrome at birth. Some children show few outward features of the condition and are born healthy. Others display many physical signs. They need medical attention right away and **therapy** for years. The number of physical features you can see does not suggest someone's level of intelligence or the kinds of sickness that may occur. Every child with Down syndrome is as different as every child without the condition.

Head and Face Features

Though each person with Down syndrome is unique, those with the condition share a certain physical appearance. Sometimes, the head is somewhat smaller than usual. The neck is shorter and may have folds in back after birth. All newborns have soft spots on their heads where bones have not grown together yet. But babies with DS have larger soft spots where

Early speech therapy helps children with Down syndrome overcome speech and language problems that may appear with the condition.

the bones may take longer to close. Skin folds and soft spots in DS infants usually disappear with age.

Most children with Down syndrome have eye openings that slant upward on the outside. The effect comes from a fold of skin called the **epicanthic fold.** The fold covers the inner corner of each eye, which creates an almond shape. The colored portion of the eye, or **iris,** may have white dots called **Brushfield spots** on the outer rim. The folds are more noticeable than the spots, but neither feature interferes with vision.

Outer ears can look different also. They may appear smaller, misshapen, or set lower on the head. Smaller ear passages make it difficult for a doctor to check inside the ears for fluid and infection. Fluid buildup blocks pathways that allow for clear hearing. As a result, many children with DS wind up with hearing loss. They need to be screened early and often to prevent hearing problems that will interfere with speech development.

Other facial features tend to be slightly smaller than those of children without Down syndrome. Smaller, flatter noses mean smaller nasal openings. This shape may lead to more frequent runny or stuffed noses. Some babies with DS are born with smaller mouths. This makes the tongue stick out and seem larger.

Many children with Down syndrome have unique tooth problems. Some teeth are slow to come out or do not come out at all. Others come in different sizes, shapes, or shades of color. So children with DS need extra dental care as they grow.

Hands and Feet

Children with Down syndrome tend to have short, thick hands and feet. The fifth finger on each hand may curve inward. A larger space than normal may develop between the first and second toes. The soles of the feet and palms of the hand usually display a single side-to-side crease, which is different from the multiple, varied creases most other people have. These features barely show, and none affect development. But the creases do create unusual fingerprints and footprints.

Muscles and Joints

Babies with Down syndrome may have weak muscles. These muscles stay so relaxed that the head and other body parts flop. Arms and legs have little strength and move too easily. Weak muscles affect general development. With exercise, muscle strength usually improves as the child ages.

Tissues around bone joints are weak, too. Weak joints are a problem, especially at the top two backbones of the neck. With these weak joints, there is a greater chance that stress on the head or neck will damage the spine. This condition can be

Reading and playing are an important part of early learning for children with Down syndrome.

corrected by surgery when a child is older. Still, doctors advise children who have this surgery to avoid most sports and heavy physical activities to prevent further stress on joints, muscle tissues, and the spine.

Mental Development

Children with Down syndrome learn to sit, walk, talk, take care of themselves, read simple books, and more. But many learn these skills more slowly than the average child. About four in five people with DS have some mental retardation. Retardation affects how babies develop overall. All babies learn from observing everything around them. But many babies with Down syndrome are slower to pick up clues from surroundings on their own. Because infants with DS have health problems, they sleep more than most babies. This causes them to miss out on much-needed contact and stimulation. With less stimulation, babies with DS may stay at one level longer than the average baby and may need extra practice to learn new skills.

OTHER HEALTH PROBLEMS

All children experience health problems. Children with Down syndrome, however, seem more likely to encounter certain difficulties. Down syndrome can produce a change in almost every system of the body. Many health concerns appear at birth, while others come later in life.

Vision Problems

Vision loss is another problem connected with Down syndrome. About three out of one hundred children with Down syndrome develop **cataracts,** a vision problem that usually occurs in adults. A cataract is a cloudy film that grows over part of the eye and blurs vision. Cataracts can be removed with surgery.

Children with Down syndrome have general vision problems. They have difficulty seeing close-up or far away. They are more likely to have crossed eyes, a condition in which one or both eyes look inward. These conditions and any vision loss from cataract surgery can often be corrected with glasses.

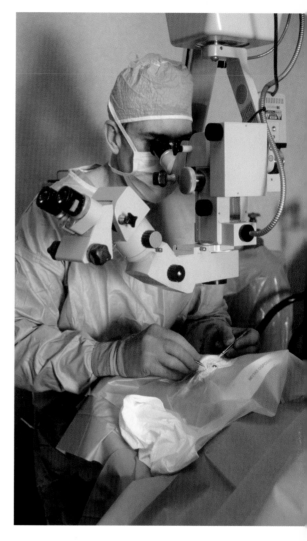

Surgery improves eyesight in people with Down syndrome who have blurry vision due to cataracts.

Hearing Loss

About three in every four children with Down syndrome wind up with mild hearing loss in at least one ear. The bones in their outer, middle, and inner ear develop abnormally before birth. This often leads to hearing difficulties. Hearing loss can stem from undetected fluid buildup in the ear or as the result of infections. Smaller ear and nose passages can cause serious infections, if not caught in time. Nowadays, medications can wipe out most infections quickly, as long as they are identified early.

These frequent ear infections may reduce the ability of a child with Down syndrome to hear sounds and words correctly. Limited hearing prevents a child from building language skills. Without fully developed speech and language, learning new skills and interacting with others are challenges for children with DS. These children benefit from speech and language therapy that helps them form sounds and learn new words.

Heart Defects

About one of every two children with Down syndrome is born with some form of heart disease. Heart defects show up in one of the four chambers of the heart or in the walls that separate these chambers. Some children are born with a hole in the wall between two chambers or in the blood vessels. Others have deformed or blocked passageways leading to and away from the heart.

Any of these problems can reduce blood supply to other parts of the body. Lowered blood supply causes someone with Down syndrome to feel more tired and less energetic than most other people. Breathing, eating, and moving become more difficult. Some heart problems in children with DS clear up over time. Doctors can correct most other problems with surgery or medication if the problems are caught early.

Digestion Problems

About one in ten babies with Down syndrome will have problems digesting food due to a birth defect associated with DS. The affected child has difficulty taking food into the body and getting rid of food waste. Often, one part of the **intestines** is blocked at birth. This means the waste cannot leave the body effectively. Doctors usually notice this problem within a week after birth. They correct it with surgery, which usually fixes the problem permanently.

Surgery on babies born with digestive problems helps them enjoy problem-free eating later on.

Seizures

Between five and ten percent of people with Down syndrome experience **seizures.** Seizures arise when normal electric charges in the brain misfire. The result can be reactions as small as a blink or as serious as total loss of body control. Seizures can last a few seconds or several minutes. With severe seizures, the body stiffens and falls, and arms and legs jerk. Sometimes, the person having a seizure drools or loses control of urine and bowel movements.

Seizures look scary and painful. But people who have them usually feel no pain. Once the seizure is over, the affected person rarely remembers what happened. Usually, he or she feels sleepy and needs to rest for a while. The main concern for anyone nearby is to remove dangerous objects from the area. This prevents injuries due to falling or thrashing during a seizure. The number of seizures increases with age. Doctors usually prescribe medication for individuals with DS who experience them.

Aging with Down Syndrome

People with Down syndrome tend to age earlier than the average population. They get old-age features and illnesses before the usual time for others their age. Gray hair and wrinkled skin may appear as early as the twenties or thirties.

Two main conditions of old age, **dementia** and **Alzheimer's disease,** often show up twenty to thirty years earlier in people with Down syndrome than in the healthy population. Dementia eventually results in memory loss. Alzheimer's disease affects the brain and all its functions as well. Besides memory loss, Alzheimer's reduces the ability to perform daily activities, such as eating and dressing. Both conditions decrease the average life span and quality of life for adults with Down syndrome.

Decades ago, children with DS were lucky to live until their first birthdays. Now life spans of fifty years and beyond are common for adults with Down syndrome. The challenge is to find ways for these adults to live free of diseases that interfere with daily living.

Advances in cell research, surgery, therapy, and infectious disease control help many people with Down syndrome to live well into adulthood.

3

THE HISTORY OF DOWN SYNDROME

The condition that we now call Down syndrome has been recognized for centuries. Pictures, writings, and science reports referred to the condition as far back as the 1500s. Yet no one identified the condition until 1866. That was when a British doctor, John Langdon Down, noticed that many babies he was treating in an institution for children with mental retardation shared certain features.

Before Down's identification, people with **disabilities** were often lumped together—and usually not for their benefit. Families often shut away their children with DS in large institutions because there was no other community support for them.

Sometimes institutions locked up children with Down syndrome with robbers, murderers, orphans, or those too poor to pay their bills. Because doctors believed they could never learn, children with DS received little education. Mostly, they were left to do nothing for most of the day. The only good news about these institutions was that they offered a lifetime of care. The bad news was that people with disabilities held little hope of getting out or seeing their families. And the care they received was often in unclean or dangerous settings.

Then new ideas about caring for disabled people developed. In the late 1800s, a few educators noticed that children who seemed slow could still make progress. In the mid-1800s, an American named Samuel Gridley Howe decided that children with disabilities needed organized education, not just protection. His ideas led to a new way of dealing

Doctor John Langdon Down, for whom Down's syndrome is named, began reforms in the treatment of mentally disabled residents in institutions.

with mental disabilities. By 1900, educators devoted a few special classes in public schools scattered across the country. Other classes for those who were retarded became part of the institutions where more of these children still lived.

RECOGNIZING DOWN SYNDROME

Doctors in the late nineteenth century also began to look more closely at people in their institutions. As they did, they noticed that many patients had similar features. A French doctor, Eduard Seguin, wrote a paper in 1866 that described children with "milk-white, rosy, and peeling skin . . . truncated (short-ened) fingers and nose; with its cracked lips and tongue. . . skin at the margin of the lids." He went on to describe the uneven walking, smaller head size, and other physical features of Down syndrome. As did Howe, Seguin urged readers to open institutions that would offer training to children with mental retardation. He was convinced that these children could learn a great deal more than previously believed. He pushed for specific activities that used the senses to encourage learning.

In that same year, John Langdon Down also published a paper. Down observed that certain children had common features beyond mental retardation. His writings may have started the myth that all children with DS are always happy. He wrote: "They have considerable power of imitation, even bordering on being mimics (imitators). They are humorous, and a lively sense of the ridiculous often colors their mimicry."

In this and another paper in 1887, Down referred to the children he described as Mongoloids. He thought their slanted eyes looked like those of people from Mongolia in Central Asia. This insulted Mongolians, but the label stuck as a scientific term until the early 1960s. During the 1960s, Asian doctors opposed the term more strongly, calling it racist. They demanded a change of thinking about the condition in both Europe and the United States. Finally, the medical community agreed. Scientists named the condition Down syndrome after the man who had described it decades earlier.

Reformers like John Langdon Down and Samuel Gridley Howe believed that life in large institutions like this one prevented people with disabilities from leading productive lives.

WHAT CAUSES DOWN SYNDROME?

Once doctors identified DS as a separate condition, they puzzled over its cause. Down had rejected the common thinking at that time—that educating women caused them to have retarded children. Instead, he blamed DS on one parent having the lung disease called tuberculosis.

Other doctors claimed to know the real reason for DS. In 1886, G. E. Shuttleworth believed Down syndrome resulted from the incomplete development of the unborn fetus. Through the years, scientists linked DS to parents who drank too much alcohol or lacked certain vitamins. Some said a lack of oxygen affected fetal cells before birth. They blamed strong drugs or X rays for causing the condition. None of these ideas proved to be the main cause of DS.

During the mid-1950s, scientists invented a more powerful microscope that enabled scientists to examine chromosomes. The first major breakthrough in the search for a cause of DS followed. In 1959, a French doctor, Jérome Lejeune, and his team studied human cells from three people with DS. When they looked at the cell under the new microscope, they discovered that chromosome pair 21 contained a third chromosome. That year, Patricia Jacobs and her team of doctors made the same discovery in England. Conclusions from both groups pointed to the finding that DS resulted from an extra chromosome in every cell of the body.

This discovery relieved parents from the guilt that they had somehow caused their child's condition. Doctors showed that

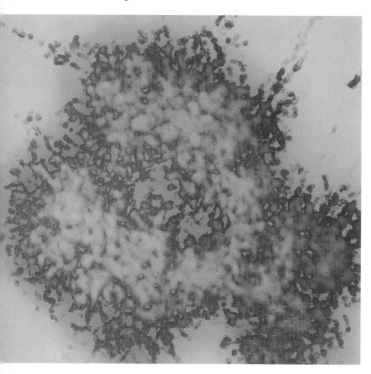

Powerful microscopes that came into use in the 1950s enabled several researchers around the world to identify abnormalities in human chromosomes.

genetic makeup was beyond a parent's control. Since this discovery, no new findings have revealed why certain cells divide incorrectly and result in DS. The exact cause of DS remains a mystery.

NEW DISCOVERIES

Exploring genes for Down syndrome led to advances in genetic science. Now scientists believe that more than one gene might cause DS. Different genes may trigger the heart defects, bone problems, cataracts, or other signs of early aging that often accompany DS.

Findings about DS sparked interest in applying gene study to other conditions. Some researchers are studying specially bred mice that serve as a model for human genetics. Using the mice, scientists are conducting research into the way genes work. Once genes are better understood, scientists hope to learn how to change them so that specific defects never occur. They hope that one day they will improve the lives of people with DS.

Scientists continue to look for clues that will unlock the secrets of DS. So far, the only known link has been the age of parents. For reasons still unknown, older parents are at greater risk of having a baby with DS. The risk of having a baby with Down syndrome is 1 in 2,000 for 20-year-old mothers. But the risk jumps to 1 in 100 for mothers over the age of 40 and even higher in mothers 45 and older. Still, most infants with DS are born to mothers under the age of 35. This is because most women tend to have babies at a younger age.

Studies also show a link between a father's age and births of babies with DS. Some scientists claim that fathers older than 50 have a greater risk of fathering a baby with DS. Scientists continue to explore the role of fathers in DS.

Some parents wonder about the likelihood of having many children with Down syndrome. But the risk of having a second baby with DS is about 1 in 100 births. The chance of having multiple children with DS increases for the small percentage of parents who carry the rare DS translocation of chromosome 21.

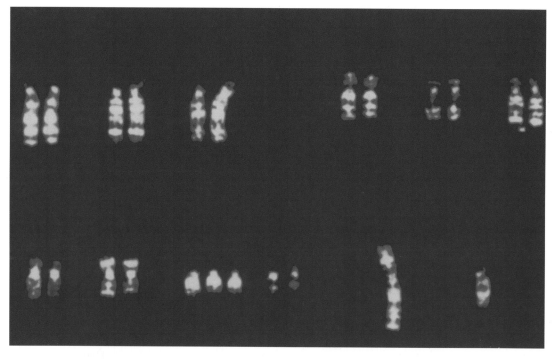

This image, called a karyotype, shows chromosomes arranged in pairs. The last row shows the extra chromosome in the twenty-first set.

Testing for Down Syndrome

Testing mothers during pregnancy helps doctors and parents prepare for the possible birth of a child with Down syndrome. Doctors usually administer the test to older mothers, mothers with older husbands, and mothers who already have a child with DS. The safest way to find out about DS before birth is to examine a sample of the mother's blood. But the blood tests do not tell the doctors that the baby has the condition. The tests only indicate the risk for having a baby with DS. Doctors order these blood tests so they can look for three possible signs that the fetus may have Down syndrome. If one of these signs is outside the normal range, additional tests are recommended to determine whether or not it is a baby with DS.

Chorionic villus sampling (CVS)—Doctors give at-risk mothers this test between 9 and 11 weeks into development. Researchers take a sample from tissue in the sac (inside the mother) that holds the fetus. Doctors obtain the sample by inserting a needle through the mother's abdomen.

Amniocentesis—This test examines a small sample of the fluid that surrounds the fetus. Doctors order this test for women who are between 14 and 18 weeks pregnant. The test determines whether cells contain an extra chromosome in the twenty-first pair.

Percutaneous umbilical blood sampling (PUBS)—This test is usually used to confirm one of the other tests. Doctors take blood from the umbilical cord, the tube that connects the fetus to the sac that surrounds it. The blood is studied for the presence of an extra chromosome.

All three tests carry some risk to the baby and mother. But doctors are trying out several new, safer tests for couples who are at high risk of having a child with DS and other genetic disorders.

A scientist who studies abnormal cell development is working on a blood test that will identify Down syndrome early in pregnancy.

4

LIVING WITH DOWN SYNDROME

My . . . [doctor] said that I would never learn and (that my parents should) send me into an institution and never see me again. No way, Jose! Mom and Dad brought me home and taught me things.

—Jason Kingsley, from his book
Count Us In: Growing Up with Down Syndrome

At one time, doctors gave parents little hope that children with Down syndrome could live with their families, go to school, and get jobs. Instead, many doctors urged parents to place their babies in institutions. Some uninformed doctors still give the same advice today. They seem unaware that a range of programs exists to help children with Down syndrome.

Most families need time to adjust to having a child with DS. This is mainly because the Down syndrome diagnosis is unexpected. New parents have certain visions of what their baby will be like. Down syndrome changes that vision. Once

Family members of a child with Down syndrome often become the child's best teachers.

families adjust to the idea of DS, they usually learn to love their babies. The child with DS brings the same joys and sorrows as any child does.

SISTERS AND BROTHERS

Down syndrome can change the kind of relationships brothers and sisters usually have. It can be difficult for them to compete with a brother or sister who is often sick or who is

Children with Down syndrome and their brothers and sisters enjoy programs that help them deal with the condition.

slower mentally. Some children take longer to adjust to having a brother or sister with DS. Sometimes being the "normal" child is difficult. They may feel pressure to be extra good so their parents will not have to worry about them. Others may do the opposite and fight or act out to get attention.

Several programs recognize that the sisters and brothers of the disabled need support, too. These programs offer activities so children can have fun without thinking about Down syndrome. The groups provide a safe place to share thoughts and feelings about living with someone who has DS.

THE LAW AND DOWN SYNDROME

Some children with DS may not need any support beyond what family, school, and communities offer any child. Others will need medical follow-up, therapy, and special school and adult services. Raising a child with DS may take extra effort. But most families agree that the benefits far outweigh the added work.

During the late 1960s and 1970s, new trends emphasized moving children with DS from institutions into the community. Many parents suddenly found themselves scrambling for training, classes, and jobs to prepare their child. Too often, they found doors closed to community programs such as camps, recreational centers, and classes.

The United States government stepped in with laws to ensure that all people with disabilities had a chance to reach their highest possible abilities. These laws granted every child the right to a good education. They guaranteed that all children receive the kind of preparation that would enable them to play useful roles in the community.

In 1973, Congress passed the Rehabilitation Act. The act became one of the first public statements against unfair treatment of people with disabilities. Section 504 addressed a child's equal opportunity. It declared that any schools, job training, or places of employment that refused to include individuals based on their disability would lose money given by the government.

In 1975, Congress passed the most far-reaching law to grant every child the right to free public schooling, the Education of the Handicapped Act, Public Law 94-142. Under this law, schools were required to offer free education to handicapped students between the ages of 3 and 21. Further, the law created guidelines for educating students with disabilities. It stated that education must suit the individual's specific needs. Classes must be part of regular situations with nondisabled children whenever fitting. In addition, a major section of the

The Education of the Handicapped Act, passed in 1975, launched school-based programs for children with disabilities like Down syndrome.

Early teaching in music, art, and reading help develop the talents of toddlers with Down syndrome.

law required teachers and therapists to meet with parents regularly to plan programs for the child. These programs were called an individualized education plan (IEP) for school-age students and an individualized family services plan (IFSP) for infants and toddlers. The law directed schools to carry out the plans and review progress regularly.

The movement to provide special and inclusive education for

Myths and Facts

Many people have outdated ideas about Down syndrome. Here are four of the most common myths:

Myth: Children with DS make better progress living in institutions than with their families.

Fact: Studies show that children who live with their families thrive beyond what was expected decades ago. The opposite is true with children raised in institutions. These children often fail to progress.

Community programs such as special education, after-school activities, and therapy, make it possible for children with Down syndrome to live full, rich lives at home with their families.

Myth: A baby with few outward signs of DS will outgrow the condition.

Fact: Down syndrome is part of a child's genetic makeup. A blood test determines the presence of DS. A baby cannot outgrow the condition. The number of DS signs depends upon the individual child.

Myth: Fewer Down syndrome features mean a baby will be smarter.

Fact: Children vary in the number and type of DS features they display. A child may or may not have any number of fifty possible DS signs and still have the condition. The number of DS signs bears no relation to a child's mental ability.

Myth: People with Down syndrome are always happy.

Fact: People with DS have the same range of feelings as those in the nondisabled population. They want to be happy, make friends, and feel they belong. They also get hurt, angry, or upset by unkind, thoughtless, or mean words or acts against them.

people with disabilities continued. In 1986, Public Law 99-457 added **early intervention** and **special education** services for disabled children ages three to five. The 1990 Individuals with Disabilities Education Act (IDEA), Public Law 101-476, expanded education services for children with disabilities further. This new law required states to explore the development of programs for babies younger than three. For older students with disabilities, the law stated that local schools must help families plan for future schooling or jobs, housing, recreation, and general adjustment to adulthood by their child's sixteenth birthday. More recently, a 2003 update required regular testing for all students—whether disabled or not.

In 1990, Congress also extended the Rehabilitation Act by passing the Americans with Disabilities Act. Besides job training and employment, the Americans with Disabilities Act promised people with disabilities equal rights to public housing, transportation, state, and local government services. This law addressed the issue of fairness in the community for the disabled population beyond school age.

Problems developed for families when each state interpreted the laws differently. States varied in the number, type, and quality of programs they offered. Even today, one state may offer a variety of programs for someone with DS. Another may provide only limited choices and no money to help meet a child's need. So families often have to fight to place their child with DS in the best setting.

Specialists work with parents to give their children with Down syndrome the best possible start in life.

EARLY INTERVENTION

Studies show that the first three years of life are the most important in any child's development. This is especially true when DS is involved. Babies with DS need early, structured programs to help parents improve their baby's physical, mental, and social abilities. These programs are called early intervention, and they should begin as early as possible, soon after birth.

Early intervention program staff members first identify a baby's strengths and weaknesses. Then they suggest a plan that suits the baby. Babies may need a onetime hearing test or ongoing physical or speech therapy. Trained staff members may come into the home and show parents exercises to perform with their child on their own. Or they may suggest that parents bring babies to a local school, clinic, or other location in the community.

Early intervention programs give parents support at a time when they are unsure about raising a child with DS. They learn how to handle and teach their baby. They may learn sign language with their child so they can communicate until speech develops. They may learn exercises to do with their baby to strengthen muscles. Just as important, the child receives needed attention when it will make the greatest difference in development—early on.

Going to School

The goal for any child is to become an independent person and citizen. Yet children with disabilities often receive fewer opportunities that would help them adjust to adulthood. Modern educators realize that children with DS need to be exposed to a range of people and situations outside the

Individualized education plans help each participating student with Down syndrome to attend special as well as mainstream classes from preschool onward.

home. In school, this means including them in classes with nondisabled children as much as possible. Educators give this idea a variety of names. Your school may call its programs "inclusion," "mainstreaming," "integrated classrooms," or something else. Whatever the name, the meaning is the same— all children, including those with Down syndrome, are part of the school community.

Inclusive or Special Classes

The individualized education plan (IEP) determines the best type of school setting for a child with Down syndrome. The IEP also states whether a student needs speech therapy or physical therapy. The setup depends upon a child's ability and behavior.

Mainstream classes like this one give a student with Down syndrome experience in dealing with many different children.

Some children with DS go to special schools. Others attend a neighborhood school in one of these types of settings:

- a class with nondisabled students.

- a class with nondisabled students and a teacher assistant or another special-education teacher to help the child with DS.

- a class with nondisabled students for part of the day and a class in another room with others who have disabilities for the rest of the day. The special class may take place in a **resource room** available for certain subjects or periods of the day. Resource room teachers have special training in working with disabled as well as nondisabled students. Some resource teachers spend part of the day with their students in the regular education classroom.

- a class with other students who have disabilities. In these classes, teachers tailor subjects to the students' needs. Subjects may include reading, writing, and math, only covered at a slower pace. Teachers may also emphasize daily living skills, such as keeping clean, dressing, and making friends. As students get older, class focus may change to training in job skills. Students learn how to deal with bosses, how to dress for work, and how to develop other job skills.

- a class with other students who have disabilities, but certain activities, often gym, art, and music, are taken with nondisabled students.

This dancer with Down syndrome participates with other children in a mainstream ballet class.

SHARING INFORMATION ABOUT DOWN SYNDROME

Sometimes, having a disability opens a person to teasing. Other students may try to take advantage of a student with Down syndrome because the child has less experience, a more trusting nature, or has not yet learned to tell right from wrong. In *Count Us In,* co-author Mitchell Levitz talks about trying so hard to fit in that he would do anything his classmates said. "When I was in ninth grade. . . I pulled the fire alarm and got suspended for five days. Because they (classmates) were telling me to do it. I just was doing it for the fun of it to get attention."

Ways to Help Someone with Down Syndrome

······································

Children with DS may learn better at home or in school if family members:

- break down activities like putting on and taking off clothes into smaller steps. Helpers can show a child with DS how to master and practice one step at a time before going on to the next so that the task is not too overwhelming.

Gentle repetition, and a lot of praise, help a child with Down syndrome learn life skills.

- repeat activities often. Most children with DS need more practice to learn new information. Repetition provides that practice and helps someone feel comfortable with learning something new.

- give praise. Everyone likes rewards for a job well done. If what you do is valued, you want to repeat what you have done. The same goes for kids with Down syndrome. Children with DS try harder when they are rewarded with praise.

- use simple language to give directions. Family and school rules need to be easy to understand.

- make sure directions are consistent and fair. Rules should apply over and over again in the same way for all family members or classmates, no matter whether they are disabled or not.

Brothers and sisters—disabled or not—help each other learn and grow.

Most teasing comes from a lack of understanding about Down syndrome. Children may feel uncomfortable with someone who stands out from everyone else. Children without disabilities may not realize that two people can be different and still have something in common. They may never have seen or met anyone with DS before.

To combat teasing, many families offer information about Down syndrome before problems occur. These parents give written information to teachers and program leaders. They may suggest a presentation to the class. During presentations, the

Special Projects

Several groups focus entirely on helping children and adults with Down syndrome use their free time in a fulfilling way.

Special Olympics. This international program provides individual and team sports training and competition for children and adults with mental retardation. The best part is that everyone is a winner. The program began in 1968 after Eunice Kennedy Shriver noticed that her campers with mental retardation were more capable in physical activities than they were given credit for. The Special Olympics expanded from her first Chicago program to 50 states and more than 100 countries.

Unified Sports. This project is an outgrowth of Special Olympics. The goal is to include people with disabilities in activities with the nondisabled. With Unified Sports, people with mental retardation play on the same team with individuals without mental retardation.

Best Buddies. Programs like Best Buddies match college students with teenagers and young adults who have disabilities. Pairs meet on a regular basis. They can talk, play sports, or watch movies—whatever activities the buddies decide on together. The main focus is on friendship.

The Special Olympics program gives challenged children and young people a place to shine in sports competition.

parent, the student with DS, or both parent and child, present facts and answer questions. They explain what it is like to have DS. They talk about how someone with DS has the same hopes, need for friends, and desire to be treated with respect that anyone has.

Sisters and brothers may get involved in such outings, too. They may have their own issues about having a brother or sister with Down syndrome. Or they may get teased about their brother or sister. So their friends and classmates may find information about DS helpful.

Equipped with new knowledge, classmates usually grow comfortable about DS. They often become more willing to invite the student with DS into their activities. Bullies lose their edge because they cannot get attention for bothering someone with DS.

With encouragement and opportunities, people with Down syndrome develop their own interests.

Some classes adopt the circle of friends idea that first started in Canada. The teacher and class discuss the included child's strengths and decide how they can encourage these abilities. Classmates share responsibility for the child throughout the day. With time, these relationships blossom into true friendships.

Developing Interests

Most children, including those with Down syndrome, have ideas about what they like to do. They enjoy playing sports, listening to music, and creating craft items. But children with DS often need encouragement to get involved in activities outside of school and work.

Communities vary in the types of activities open to children with DS. Park districts offer a range of classes, lessons, and team sports. Some special education districts pool their funds to offer recreational activities for people with disabilities after school, on weekends, and during summers. Boy Scouts and Girl Scouts organize troops with disabled and nondisabled members. People with DS can participate in programs through the YWCA, YMCA, and religious organizations.

Young Adults with Down Syndrome

Studies show that teenagers with DS experience the same physical changes as in the nondisabled population. They also

Employees with Down syndrome work in a variety of workplaces with and without special supervision.

have the same need to fit in. But they may be less able to understand what is happening to their bodies. Teens with DS need specific instruction about what is normal and what is private or public. They must learn that boys' and girls' bodies change as they get older. Role-playing, where people act out situations, is one way to help teens with Down syndrome learn how to deal with new situations. Role-playing helps them practice how to act with friends, greet a stranger, or conduct a job interview.

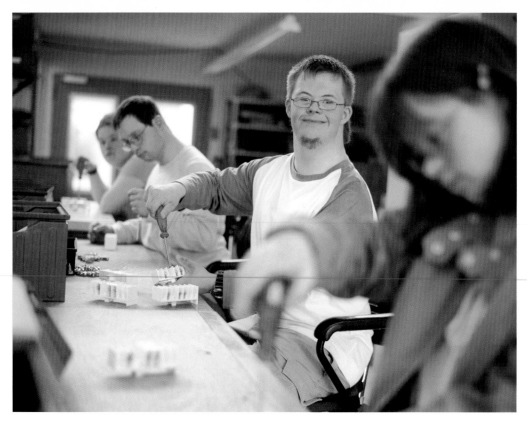
These workers are assembling machine parts in a sheltered job setting.

AFTER SCHOOL

People with Down syndrome display a range of interests, skills, and talents similar to those in the rest of the population. A few teens with DS do go to college. Most find jobs. But job choices may be limited by the person's physical skills, ability to pay attention, work safely, and travel to and from work.

Federal, state, and local agencies try to offer a variety of employment choices, such as:

• *Competitive employment.* This is a full-time or part-time job in a regular work setting. The worker receives wages and performs a job alongside nondisabled people.

- *Supported employment.* This is work in a regular setting. But employees with Down syndrome receive ongoing help on the job. In some programs, a job coach teaches job tasks and monitors the disabled workers. In others, the worker is part of a crew with disabilities that travels to various work sites to perform simple jobs, such as groundskeeping or housecleaning services.
- *Sheltered employment.* In this situation, the person with Down syndrome performs together with others who have disabilities. People may work in a sheltered workshop, a work activity center, or an adult daycare program. Staff members train the workers for jobs that come from community industries. Workers receive constant supervision from staff trained to work with adults who have disabilities. The work may include packaging, assembling, or sewing. Other tasks may be stuffing envelopes or packages. Everyone in the workshop performs the same task. Workers are paid a small amount for each completed item.

Adults with fewer skills stay in programs that concentrate on social, daily living, and recreation skills. These workers receive no pay.

Living Arrangements

Until recently, independent housing choices for adults with retardation have been limited. To find housing, residents moved far from their neighborhoods and families. This cut them off from the communities they knew. Now creative choices allow more adults with Down syndrome to live near their families. Some house only residents with DS. Other settings house residents with other disabilities as well as those with Down syndrome. The range of options depends upon how independent someone can be and what the community offers.

Twenty-four-hour-care programs are for adults who cannot take care of themselves. Staff members supervise everything from daytime programs to dressing, eating, and participating in free-time activities. Another type of housing in communities may include group homes. These homes or buildings have live-in support staff members who coordinate the activities of residents. Residents may go to work, adult daycare, or other programs outside the home.

Semi-independent apartments provide a similar setting. In an apartment situation, adults live alone or with a small group of residents. They may hold jobs during the day and take part in after-work social activities. A staff person either lives nearby or checks in regularly.

Some independent adults with Down syndrome live and work totally on their own. This is the dream parents have for all their children. This dream is no different when Down syndrome is involved. As Jason Kingsley wrote, "Give a baby with a disability a chance to grow a full life. To experience a half-full glass instead of the half-empty glass. And think of your abilities, not your disability."

Group homes for adults with Down syndrome and other disabilities make it possible for them to live near their families.

Reaching for the Stars

Like all people, those with Down syndrome have dreams and many made those dreams come true.

Chris Burke, actor and author: Thirty-three-year-old Burke has acted in movies and on television. His landmark role as Corky in the television series, *Life Goes On* earned him a Golden Globe nomination. He has guest-starred on several other shows and has written an autobiography, *A Special Kind of Hero*. He has been a spokesperson for the National Down Syndrome Congress, National Down Syndrome Society, and ARC, encouraging others who have DS. Always positive, he was one of the first people to call Down syndrome "Up syndrome."

Molly Sosnowski, Special Olympic athlete: Molly Sosnowski first learned to ski at age six. She has participated in the Special Olympics since 1991. In 2005, at age 27, she represented Team USA at the Special Olympics World Games in Nagano, Japan. Sosnowski is a world champ, and came in second, fourth, and fifth in her three intermediate downhill events.

Jason Kingsley, author, actor: Jason Kingsley could read at age four, later could count to ten in twelve different languages, and also appeared on *Sesame Street*. By the time he reached age 24, he had graduated from a full high school program and had voted in a presidential election. He also co-authored *Count Us In: Growing Up with Down Syndrome* with his friend Mitchell Levitz, who also has Down syndrome. Kingsley lives and works on his own, and has acted in several television shows. He also spoke regularly to groups about the importance of encouraging children and adults with DS.

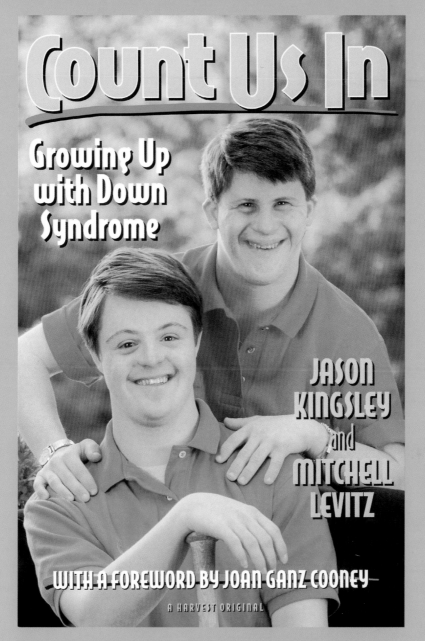

Count Us In

Growing Up with Down Syndrome

JASON KINGSLEY and MITCHELL LEVITZ

WITH A FOREWORD BY JOAN GANZ COONEY

A HARVEST ORIGINAL

Despite his disabilities, Jason Kingsley (shown here in the blue shirt) has been able to make his dreams come true.

GLOSSARY

Alzheimer's disease—A disease that affects the brain, causing severe memory loss.

Brushfield spots—The white dots on the outer rim of the iris of eyes. The dots often appear in Down syndrome.

cataracts—The cloudy film that covers the lenses of eyes and causes blurred vision.

cells—The smallest living parts of the body.

chromosomes—The parts of human body cells that carry genes.

dementia—A condition that involves the worsening of memory, thinking skills, and behaviors.

disability—The inability to do something because of a problem with the body, mind, or emotions.

early intervention—A program for children from birth to age three that helps lessen the effects of disabilities.

epicanthic fold—A fold of skin that covers the inner corner of each eye in an individual with DS.

fetus—A developing unborn human or other mammal.

genes—The tiny rod-shaped structures inside cells. Genes determine traits of an organism and are passed on from parent to child.

human genetics—The basic makeup of the body.

intestines—The digestive tube that runs from the stomach to where waste leaves the body.

iris—The colored portion of the eye.

mental retardation—The reduced rate of learning that causes difficulty in reasoning, remembering, and putting ideas together.

mosaicism—A form of Down syndrome caused by cells that contain mixed types of genetic material.

resource room—A separate classroom that is available to a special education teacher who teaches students with disabilities.

seizures—The unusual electrical discharges in the brain that trigger a range of movements.

special education—The kind of teaching used for children who have disabilities.

syndrome—A set of physical signs that appear together in a person and point to a particular condition.

therapists—The people trained in methods of treatment for a physical or mental condition.

therapy—The treatment to improve social behavior or the use of one or more parts of the body.

tissues—The material made up of cells of which an organism is made.

translocation—The movement of a faulty chromosome containing extra genetic material to another cell.

trisomy—A form of Down syndrome caused by an extra copy of chromosome 21.

FIND OUT MORE

ORGANIZATIONS

The Arc of the United States
(formerly the National Association for Retarded Citizens)
1010 Wayne Ave., Suite 650
Silver Spring, MD 20910
800-433-5255
www.thearc.org

Family Resource Center on Disabilities
20 E. Jackson Blvd., Room 300
Chicago, IL 60604
312-939-3513
www.frcd.org

National Down Syndrome Congress
1370 Center Drive, Suite 102
Atlanta, GA 30338
800-232-6372 or 770-604-9500
www.ndsccenter.org

National Down Syndrome Society
666 Broadway
New York, NY 10012
800-221-4602
www.ndss.org

BOOKS

Bowman-Kruhm, Mary. *Everything You Need to Know About Down Syndrome*. New York: Rosen Publishing Group, 2000.

Brandt, Caroline. *He Has Up Syndrome, Not Down Syndrome* Frederick, MD: Publish America, 2005.

Burke, Chris, and Skotkey, Brian. *A Special Kind of Hero: Chris Burke's Own Story* New York: Doubleday, 1991.

Kidder, Cynthia, and McDaniel, Jo Beth. *Common Threads: Celebrating Life with Down Syndrome*. Rochester, Hills, MI: Band of Angels Press, 2001.

Kingsley, Jason, and Levitz, Mitchell. *Count Us In: Growing Up with Down Syndrome*. New York: Harcourt Brace, 1994.

Royston, Angela. *Down Syndrome*. Chicago: Heinemann, 2005.

Web Sites

Down Syndrome for Kids
http://www.kidshealth.org/kid/health_problems/birth_defect/
   down_syndrome.html

National Council on Disability (NCD)
www.ncd.gov

Soda Pop Online: Siblings of Disabled (Kids) and Peers Offering
Promise
www.sodapoponline.org

Zigawhat! Connect with Other Kids
www.nichcy.org/kids

INDEX

Page numbers for illustrations are in **boldface**

aging, 22, 29
Alzheimer's disease, 22, 23
Americans with Disabilities Act, 39
amniocentesis, 31

Best Buddies, 48
blood tests, 31, **31,** 38
bones, 14, 17, 19, 29
Brushfield spots, 15
Burke, Chris 56

cataracts, 19, **19,** 20, 29
cell division, **13,** 14, 29
Chorionic villus sampling (CVS), 31
chromosomes, 12, 13, 14, **28,** 30, **30,** 31
dementia, 22, 23
digestive problems, 21, **21**
Down, John Langdon, 24, **25,**26, 27,**27**

early intervention, 39, 40
ears, 15, 19
education, 24, 25, 35, 37, 39
Education of the Handicapped Act, 36, **36**
employment, 52, 53
epicanthic fold, 15
eyes, 10, 15, 20
        See also vision problems

feet, 16
fetus, 11, 27, 31

genes, 11, 12, 29, 38

hands, 16
hearing problems, 16, 19, 20
heart problems, 8, 20, 21, 29
history, 24-31, **25, 27**

housing, 53, 54, **55**
Howe, Samuel Gridley, 25, 26, **27**

inclusion, 42-44
Individualized Education Plan (IEP), 37, **42,** 43
Individualized Family Services Plan, 37, **42**
Individuals with Disabilities Act (IDEA), 39

Jacobs, Patricia, 28
joints, 17, 18

karyotype, **30**
Kingsley, Jason, 54, 56, **56**

language, 19, 46
        therapy, 20
Lejeune, Jerome, 28
Levitz, Mitchell, 45, 56
life span, 23

mainstreaming, 42, **43, 45**
        See also inclusion
mental retardation, 10, 18, 26, 48
Mongoloids, 26
mosaicism, 13
muscles, 8, 13, 17, 41
myths, 38

National Down Syndrome Congress, 56
National Down Syndrome Society, 10, 56
nose, 16, 19

parents, 6-9, 28-32, 34-37, **40,** 46, 49, 54
        older parents 29, 30
percutaneous umbilical blood sampling (PUBS), 31
        See also Blood tests
physical features, 6-7, **11,** 14–18, 38

Rehabilitation Act, 35, 39

Seguin, Eduard, 26
seizures, 22
Shriver, Eunice Kennedy, 48
Shuttleworth, G. E., 27
siblings, 33, 34, **34**, 46, **47,** 49
sign language, 8, 9, 41
Sosnowski, Molly, 56, **56**
special education, 37, **38,** 39, 50
Special Olympics, 9, 48, **48,** 56
speech, 15, 19
      therapy, 20, 41

spine, 17, 18

teeth, 16
tissues, 17, 18
toes, 16
translocation, 13, 30
trisomy, 13

Unified Sports, 48
vision problems, 19
      See also cataracts

Web sites, 61, 62

ABOUT THE AUTHOR

Marlene Targ Brill writes about many topics, from history and biography to sports, world peace, and tooth fairies. Her favorite topics involve ways to help people understand each other better. That is part of what she did when she taught children who had special needs, like those with Down syndrome. She helped her students progress. But she also played a large role in helping others understand that children with disabilities were more like them than different. Now she writes about special needs in books for children and for adults. Marlene lives near Chicago with her husband, Richard, and daughter, Alison.